Alex David

EXAMINING

"GIVE ME LIBERTY OR GIVE ME DEATH"

BY PATRICK HENRY

Published in 2021 by Enslow Publishing, LLC
101 W. 23rd Street, Suite 240, New York, NY 10011

Library of Congress Cataloging-in-Publication Data

Names: David, Alex, author.
Title: Examining "Give me liberty or give me death" by Patrick Henry / Alex David.
Description: New York : Enslow Publishing, 2021. | Series: American debates and speeches | Audience: Grades: 6-12. | Includes bibliographical references and index.
Identifiers: LCCN 2019013024| ISBN 9781978515079 (library bound) | ISBN 9781978515062 (pbk.)
Subjects: LCSH: Henry, Patrick, 1736-1799—Juvenile literature. | Henry, Patrick, 1736-1799—Oratory—Juvenile literature. | United States. Continental Congress—Biography—Juvenile literature. | Legislators—United States—Biography—Juvenile literature. | Speeches, addresses, etc., American—History and criticism—Juvenile literature. | United States—Politics and government—1775-1783—Juvenile literature.
Classification: LCC E302.6.H5 D38 2021 | DDC 973.3092 [B] —dc23
LC record available at https://lccn.loc.gov/2019013024

Printed in the United States of America

To Our Readers: We have done our best to make sure all websites in this book were active and appropriate when we went to press. However, the author and the publisher have no control over and assume no liability for the material available on those websites or on any websites they may link to. Any comments or suggestions can be sent by email to customerservice@enslow.com.

Portions of this book originally appeared in *Patrick Henry's Liberty or Death Speech* by Jesse Jarnow.

Photos Credits: Photo research by Bruce Donnola

Cover, pp. 1, 23 Fotosearch/Archive Photos/Getty Images; p. 5 Stock Montage/Archive Photos/ Getty Images; p. 8 Jason O. Watson/historical-markers.org/Alamy Stock Photo; p. 9 Zack Frank/ Shutterstock.com; pp. 10, 14 Universal History Archive/Universal Images Group/Getty Images; p. 17 Copyright © Gerry Embleton/North Wind Picture Archives; p. 18 Yale Center for British Art, Paul Mellon Collection, USA/Bridgeman Images; p. 25 Stock Montage/Archive Photos/Getty Images; p. 26 Everett Historical/Shutterstock.com; pp. 29, 31 MPI/Archive Photos/Getty Images; p. 35 Ken Welsh/Perspectives/Getty Images; p. 36 Heritage Images/Hulton Archive/Getty Images; pp. 39, 47 Universal Images Group/Getty Images; p. 43 Military PCF/Alamy Stock Photo; p. 44 Michael Rega/Shutterstock.com; p. 50 GraphicaArtis/Archive Photos/Getty Images; Ozz Design/ Shutterstock.com (back cover and interior pages background pattern); pashabo/Shutterstock. com (interior pages American flag patterns); Midwaves/Shutterstock.com, Leonid Zarubin/ Shutterstock.com (interior pages abstract textures and patterns)

CONTENTS

INTRODUCTION

There were 120 delegates from all over the country who sat in St. John's Church on March 23, 1775. Whispers of revolution were blowing across the colonies. An independent America was an idea and a hopeful experiment.

Thomas Jefferson and George Washington sat in the audience that day, as a young lawyer got up from his pew and stood in front of his countrymen. Outside it was fiercely cold, but inside it was stuffy. Ideas and discomfort tangled together as the men sat in the cramped church. They opened the windows to let in a cold, spring breeze.

Patrick Henry began to speak. His mellifluous voice wafted upward among the rafters. He was known as being a radical and someone able to persuade people with his voice. He said, "I have but one lamp by which my feet are guided, and that is the lamp of experience."

This was the Virginia Convention. It was a three day conference where these people would decide what to do. Should they revolt against King George? Were they tired enough of his taxes and unfair treatment of the colonists? Or should they continue to be a colony under England?

Government at this time was often thought of as being guided by God. Kings were picked not by the people, but

Patrick Henry, painted here, lived from 1736 to 1799.

by God. The idea of democracy, of government serving the people's voice, was not a common idea.

Patrick Henry's neck began to tighten as he talked. His youth was spent reenacting the preacher of his church and it was evident in both his delivery and the content of his speech that he was greatly influenced by religion.

There is no longer any room for hope. If we wish to be free—if we mean to preserve inviolate those inestimable privileges for which we have been so long contending—if we mean not basely to abandon the noble struggle in which we have been so long engaged, and which we have pledged ourselves never to abandon until the glorious object of our contest shall be obtained—we must fight! I repeat it, sir, we must fight! An appeal to arms and to the God of hosts is all that is left us!

Henry punctuated his speech with long periods of silence and then he would throw his voice, booming out into the crowd. He held his hands up to the colonists and made his wrists look shackled. He urged them to fight to release the chains of slavery. England shouldn't have this strong a hold on them.

Henry grabbed a nearby letter opener with his hands, "I know not what course others may take," he said, his voice booming, practically shouting. He mimicked plunging the letter opener into his heart, "but as for me, give me liberty or give me death."

The other men were startled awake, ready. These words helped begin a war. A revolution. Soldiers would stitch this phrase into their uniforms: Give me liberty or give me death. Patrick Henry was the voice of that revolution.

CHAPTER ONE

REBEL WITH A CAUSE

I n the late spring of 1736, Patrick Henry was born in Hanover, County Virginia. He was born at home to his mother, Sarah, and his father, John. His parents named him after his uncle, the Reverend Patrick Henry.

Virginia was a colony at the time. This was before America had states. It was land occupied by indigenous persons and these new transplants called Americans. The colonies in 1736 were ruled by King George II, but would soon, in 1760, be ruled by King George III, the king who the Americans would later revolt against.

An Untamed Wilderness

The colonies were officially under the control of the British Empire. However, life in the colonies bore little resemblance to life in England. It was relatively backward. There were no huge cities, and there were few outlets for cultural expression. There was untamed wilderness everywhere. Also, the social order was less established in comparison to England's. To many, there was nothing but untapped potential. To Patrick's dad, John Henry, and others like him, America offered a new way of life. If one opportunity didn't work out, a person could simply seek out another.

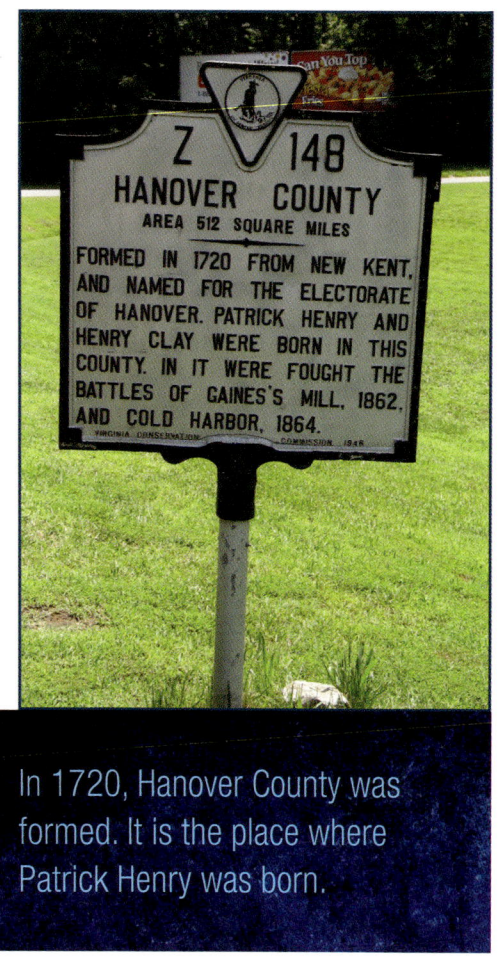

In 1720, Hanover County was formed. It is the place where Patrick Henry was born.

John and Sarah schooled their children at home. Young Patrick received a basic classical education, learning some Latin and Greek, as well as other rudiments. With eight other children to raise, the Henry family struggled to make ends meet.

Mastering the Art of Oration

When Patrick was a child, Hanover County was in the grip of a religious revival. Itinerant Presbyterian and Baptist preachers passed through with frequency. Patrick's grandfather, Isaac Winston, was one of the first to be won over by these preachers. Though religious tolerance was practiced elsewhere in the colonies, it was harder to come by in backwoods Virginia. Most people there subscribed to the beliefs of the Anglican church, which was the Church of England. To them, doing otherwise was blasphemy (being disrespectful to God). Instead of attending an Anglican church, Winston and others participated in private Bible reading groups. Winston hosted traveling preachers in his home.

As a child, Patrick Henry loved being outdoors. America, at the time, was a great wilderness.

He was persecuted for it. He had to pay fines to the local government, which regarded the practice of a non-Anglican faith as a disturbance of the peace.

Learning to Preach

Nonetheless, the preachers kept coming. In 1745, George Whitefield, the most famous of the revivalists, came through Hanover County. Young Patrick watched him with interest. Two years later, Reverend Samuel Davies, a Presbyterian, moved to Hanover County. Though less famous than Whitefield, he would have a much greater influence on Patrick. Sarah Henry, Patrick's mother, took him to see Davies speak many times.

George Whitefield, pictured above, preached during the Great Awakening, when thousands of new Americans converted to Evangelicalism.

Bird Calls

In the 1720s, John Syme, a friend of Patrick's dad, built Studley, what would later be Patrick's home. A large tobacco plantation swept across the land. Cicadas chirped in the distance. Wind rustled the trees. As a boy, Patrick was in love with nature. Patrick was attuned to sound from an early age. He would walk the land outside his house, listening to the sounds of nature. He was intrigued by the melodies of birdsongs and would often copy their songs. This vocal control would come in handy in his later life when his voice rang for freedom.

Davies was a masterful orator. He spoke with conviction. His words soared from his mouth and resounded through the church. Davies had a masterful control of his voice. He brought it from a delicate whisper to booming heights. Depending on his sermon, he could sound frightened, angry, or even like he was singing.

During the carriage rides home, Sarah would ask Patrick to repeat Davies's sermons. Soon, he was able to imitate Davies's voice. Though Patrick was never religiously converted by Davies, he found him a remarkable inspiration. Later, he would call Davies the greatest speaker he had ever seen. To join a non-Anglican church was an act of protest against the old ways. In being so profoundly influenced by Davies, Patrick was inherently anti-British from a young age.

Just as much as Patrick was shaped by his experiences seeing Reverend Davies, he was also shaped by experiences with his father. John Henry was quite active in the local Anglican church. But the local church meant far more than religion. Men would arrive early and discuss business and politics in the churchyard. They talked about the current prices of various crops. They bet on horse races and cockfights. After the service, Patrick and his father would spend the day in town. Patrick vastly enjoyed these Sundays. They gave Patrick his first taste of a life in which politics, business, and religion were combined. These experiences deeply shaped the kind of politician Patrick would one day become.

The Path to Law

In 1754, Patrick Henry married Sarah Sallie Shelton, the daughter of John Shelton, a wealthy farmer. As Sarah's wedding dowry, John Shelton gave the couple 600 acres (242 hectares) of land, a house called Pine Slash, and six slaves. Though Henry had never farmed before, he threw himself into the task of working the land. Unfortunately, it was a bad year for farmers throughout Virginia. A drought in the summer and an early frost in the fall caused Henry's tobacco crop to fail miserably. The next year, fire destroyed his house.

John Shelton took pity on the young couple, who by now had their first child. He arranged for them to move into the Hanover Tavern, where Henry was made barkeeper. Henry soon opened another store just outside of town. This time he was more successful. The tavern was across the street from Hanover Court House, and it attracted business from lawyers on their way to and from court. The lawyers also shopped at his store. Henry often overheard them arguing about the law, and their discussions intrigued him. Soon, he developed an interest in law. With a single-minded determination, he decided to become a lawyer in 1760.

In the eighteenth century, there were fewer requirements for becoming a lawyer than there are today. Although American law was based on British law, the necessities of the new land often required great flexibility. Everything about the American colonies was less formal. Many judges were learned laymen whose services were needed only occasionally. Frequently, legal decisions were based more on common sense than on legal precedent, or established law.

For prospective lawyers, this was good news. Instead of years of legal training, a man needed only to have a good head on his shoulders. In Virginia, law candidates needed to pass an oral examination given by a panel of attorneys. The examination would evaluate a candidate's abilities by engaging him in theoretical arguments about the law. Henry set to work studying. Since his days watching Reverend Davies, his speaking skills had improved. Now, he simply needed knowledge of the law. He paid closer attention to lawyers' conversations in the tavern. He asked many questions. Many recommended a book entitled *Institutes of the Laws of England* by Sir Edward Coke, which outlined how common law had developed in England.

In April 1760, Henry rode two days to Williamsburg to undergo his oral exam by a panel of Virginia's most respected lawyers. Though the well-respected John Randolph was put off by Henry's rough appearance, he was won over by his debating

John Randolph, painted here by Gilbert Stuart, was one of Virginia's best educated lawyers. He would later become the attorney general of Virginia.

skills. Having passed the examination, Henry became a lawyer. He rode from county to county to present his certification. Gradually, he built up a list of clients. For the next three years, Henry went from courthouse to courthouse. He dealt with credit cases. He wrote wills. Though the cases were small, he quickly built a reputation as a man of the people. Henry spoke in a way that was simultaneously elegant and understandable.

The Parson's Case

In 1763, Henry argued in the so-called Parson's Cause case, which made him famous. Henry represented local farmers and officials. They were sued by members of the English clergy in Virginia to recover back pay after King George II overturned the Two Penny Act. Before the Two Penny Act was passed, the clergy was paid in tobacco. The law had allowed locals to pay the clergy with money, but at a rate that was lower than the market price of tobacco. Henry argued passionately in court, unleashing his full powers. During his final argument, he let loose with a wildly breathless torrent of words. He declared that the king of England had "degenerated into a tyrant." The audience went mad. It stood cheering. The judge pounded his gavel to little avail. When order was restored, he ruled in favor of Henry's clients. Farmers carried Henry out of the courtroom on their shoulders in celebration.

Patrick Henry was beginning to understand the power of speech. Around him, America was starting to question their relationship to the king. The colonies were having to pay taxes to a king that did not truly represent them. Patrick Henry positioned himself to be the voice that urged his fellow Americans to revolt.

CHAPTER TWO

TAXATION WITHOUT REPRESENTATION

Tensions began between England and this new America. First, Great Britain was very far away. Because of distance, cultures were growing apart. America was more similar to a frontier than the regimented society of England. Second, England's economy was declining, whereas the colonists were finding ways to be quite prosperous. In Virginia, tobacco profits were booming. The colonists were becoming increasingly independent. Members of British Parliament were uncomfortable with their growing freedom. The colonists were beginning to see themselves as wholly separate, not wanting to be part of a system that didn't represent them. The colonies were like children that Mother England was having less and less control over.

England's Debt

Throughout much of the eighteenth century, England was engaged in a series of military conflicts known as the Imperial Wars. These wars were fought primarily among England, Spain, and France to gain or hold territories in the Americas. The last

The new Americans' culture was becoming increasingly different from England's culture.

of these wars was the French and Indian War (1754–1763). Waged between England and France for control of the Ohio territory, the war lasted nine years and took place entirely in North America. England fared well in the Imperial Wars, and the British Empire grew as a result. However, its success came at a high price. By the end of the hostilities in 1763, England was deeply in debt.

At the conclusion of the French and Indian War, England turned its attention to exercising tighter control over its colonies and reducing its debt. To meet these goals, it made a number

Culture in England valued tradition and hierarchy. Those in America valued survival in the unexplored wilderness.

of decisions that were resisted by the American colonists. First, with the Proclamation of 1763, King George III tried to alleviate hostilities between the colonists and American Indians by prohibiting the colonists from moving westward into territory still populated by the Indians. Next, the British parliament decided to place a large permanent army throughout its empire and to institute new taxes on the colonies to pay for it. The army was to consist of twenty regiments, each made up of approximately 1,000 soldiers.

Angry Americans

As angered as the colonists were by these actions, it was a series of laws passed by Parliament in 1764 and 1765 that sparked the independence movement leading to the American Revolution. The Sugar Act of 1764 lowered the existing tax

The Currency of the Colonies

Money in the new colonies was haphazard. England used an organized bimetallic system, which meant they exchanged gold and silver coins for currency. These coins were called specie. However, the colonies did not use specie and currency varied across each colony. The most common currency was Spanish coins, as colonists used this money in their trade with the West Indies. From 1643-1660 in Massachusetts, people traded in wampum or shells that the Native Americans used. In Virginia and North Carolina, tobacco leaves were also used as legal tender. Eventually the colonists used paper notes that represented not gold or silver, but the colonies' greatest commodity: land.

on sugar products, but established strict procedures to make sure that the taxes were collected. The Currency Act of 1764 banned the issuing of colonial currency. The Stamp Act of 1765 placed a tax on many paper goods, including commercial and legal documents. Finally, the Quartering Act required colonists to provide housing and various household necessities for members of the permanent army.

The reaction to these laws—to the Stamp Act in particular—was explosive. Individuals regarded the new laws as attempts to weaken their personal liberties. Businessmen saw them as affronts to their financial liberties, as well as obstructions to trade. Colonists from all walks of life worked to block the implementation of the new laws and eventually overturn them. Ordinary citizens protested in the streets and in government buildings. Some activists even shut down colonial courts to prevent the use of certain stamps. Merchants and consumers boycotted English goods. Colonial legislatures passed resolutions denouncing the laws and establishing obstacles to the collection of the taxes. In addition, political, religious, and business leaders began debating whether the laws violated the British Constitution.

No Longer British Subjects

Patrick Henry witnessed much of this firsthand. His rounds took him from county to county, where he saw the resistance. He could see that the colonists were developing a new identity that emphasized their American culture over their legal status as British subjects. Certain words began to cross the lips of these new Americans: Freedom. Liberty.

Many of the leaders of the American resistance were wealthy businessmen. While surely they believed in personal freedoms, much of their anger was fueled by money. In the next years, they worked to mobilize the lower classes toward revolution.

Nowhere was this better embodied than in Virginia's House of Burgesses (the colony's house of representatives), which Henry joined in 1765. It was made up predominantly of wealthy Virginians. Henry was neither rich nor experienced. He was admitted to the House of Burgesses mostly based on the fame of his speech in the Parson's Cause case. As a member of the House of Burgesses, he played a role in many of the important issues of the day.

Henry arrived for his first session on May 20, 1765, when the Stamp Act was the hot topic throughout the colonies. But nobody would raise the issue for discussion during the official proceedings of the House. It was too controversial. The governor had threatened to dissolve the House if any member even brought it up. Instead, members met to discuss the Stamp Act in taverns and hotels. Wisely, they waited for the last day of the session to discuss it on the floor of the House. They wished to lodge an official complaint against the British government. Several members wrote a resolution. Impressed by Henry's eloquence, they asked him to speak for them in the House. He agreed.

Henry's speech was aggressive. As with the Parson's Cause, he voiced what many had been thinking, but few had the courage to say. As in other political bodies, arguments in the House of Burgesses frequently rested on a knowledge of history. In speeches, members would cite legal precedents and obscure sources. Henry had none of that. He said simply that he believed that a good American would stand up against tyranny. At the word "tyranny," John Robinson, the Speaker of the House who oversaw the proceedings, bristled. "Treason!" he shouted. "Treason!"

The resolution didn't pass. It was too strongly worded. But it was a close vote—so close that it was misreported in several places to have passed. Several Virginia newspapers printed the entire resolution. Word spread around the colonies. Many people were inspired by Henry's inflammatory remarks.

Britain Backs Down

In October, representatives from nine colonies met in New York for the Stamp Act Congress. They approved a set of fourteen resolutions, which were sent to England, protesting the Stamp Act on constitutional grounds. They argued that under the British Constitution, the colonists, as British subjects, could be taxed only by their elected representatives. Accordingly, because the colonies were not represented in Parliament, it lacked the power to tax them.

The following year, Parliament repealed the Stamp Act. This was more in response to the colonists' boycott of British goods than to their constitutional arguments. In fact, Parliament passed the Declaratory Act of 1766, reasserting its authority to make laws to regulate the colonies in all matters. It also punished New York's legislative body for violating the Quartering Act by taking away its right to pass legislation.

Patrick Henry speaks to the House of Burgesses.

Townshend Revenue Act

In the next years, tension increased dramatically between England and the American colonies. In 1767, Parliament imposed a new set of taxes on the colonies with the Townshend Revenue Act. Again, the colonies resisted the new act. By the late 1760s, the new taxes were bringing in increasingly higher revenue. However, it did little to offset the costs of keeping a standing army in the colonies.

The Boston Massacre

Riots and protests broke out with some consistency, to which Parliament often responded by strengthening its forces in the trouble spots. In 1770, British soldiers shot and killed several Boston citizens who had pelted them with snowballs during a protest against the Quartering Act. The incident, which became known as the Boston Massacre, further inflamed anti-British sentiment among the colonists.

By this time a familiar pattern had developed in the relation-ship between England and the colonies. The colonies responded to British attempts to regulate them with organized opposition. This in turn led England to punish the offending colonies by taking away some of their legislative rights or stationing more troops there. The breaking point came in 1774, in the wake of the Boston Tea Party, during which Boston residents dumped 90,000 pounds (40,823 kilograms) of tea, belonging to the British East India Company, into Boston Harbor. They were protesting against the newly instituted Tea Act, which gave the company a monopoly on the sale of tea in the colonies.

The Boston Massacre, which occurred on March 5, 1770, is illustrated here.

The Intolerable Acts

In response, Parliament passed the Coercive Acts—the Intolerable Acts to the colonists—to punish Massachusetts. The laws closed Boston Harbor, declared that British troops could be housed in private homes, took back the Boston colonists' right to select its legislators, and authorized the Massachusetts royal governor to send officials and soldiers accused of crimes outside of the colony to be tried. All across the colonies, people were outraged. The other colonies rallied in support of Massachusetts.

The thirteen colonies had been largely separated. The Massachusetts Bay Colony was much different than Virginia. The people in Massachusetts were religious, as it was originally founded by the Puritans who were looking for religious freedom. Virginia, or the Chesapeake Bay Colony as it was called, was largely focused on profit. The colony used tobacco to make their profit. The colonies were so separate that Benjamin Franklin drew a disembodied snake with each colony as a section. He wrote the words "Join, or Die" underneath.

Benjamin Franklin created what some consider America's first political cartoon. Each segment of the disembodied snake symbolizes the colony.

An American

However, in September of 1774, the First Continental Congress met in Philadelphia. Patrick Henry made the arduous journey from Virginia to be at the meeting. He was the first speaker and he said, "I am not a Virginian, but an American!"

The colonies recognized the need to identify as one, larger unit that would be able to fight against England if the time came. At this meeting, the delegates did not pass a motion for independence—they were one vote short, but they still unified. However, Patrick Henry, in tune with the mood of the times, knew that England was preparing for battle.

CHAPTER THREE

THE VOICE OF REVOLUTION

The Continental Congress was an important part of pre-revolution America. In 1774, because it was a colony, there was no national government. The Continental Congress became the center of resistance to British rule. In response to Britain's oppressive Intolerable Acts the Continental Congress created the Articles of Association which stated that the Americans would boycott British goods starting on December 1, 1774.

The colonists began to make as much of their own goods as possible. They refused to buy cloth from England and held spinning parties at their homes. The women at Patrick's home used a loom to make their own cloth. They spun cotton into clothes for his family and for the slaves. However, amongst the resistance, colonists were beginning to be afraid of the British redcoats that walked the streets. Colonists wondered if they would be prepared if war were to happen. During this time, the First Continental Congress was careful to not criticize the king directly, but rather say how unhappy they were with the current situation. Additionally, the Articles of Association told

On September 5, 1774, the First Continental Congress met in Philadelphia.

colonists how to act during the boycott. They urged people not to have cockfights, not to have expensive plays or buy expensive mourning clothes after the death of a family member.

Raising a Militia in the Colonies

In December, Maryland established a militia, a local army. A typical militia was comprised of a colony's free male inhabitants between the ages of sixteen and fifty. Militiamen armed themselves and met regularly to practice. Marylanders wanted their militia to be ready for any emergency. Henry followed these activities with great interest. He believed that Virginia, too, needed a militia.

Other high-powered Virginians agreed with him. In January 1775, George Washington and George Mason began to

Secret Club

In 1765, colonists were so angry at Britain that some formed a secret club called the Sons of Liberty. It started in Boston and lasted until 1776. The group was originally made up of nine tradesmen and merchants, but it quickly grew. Soon, every colony had members. Their main objective was to scare tax collectors, who enforced the Stamp Act, to resign. The group was responsible for the Boston Tea Party. Just like Patrick Henry, the group relied on words to change people's minds. They used newspaper articles to convince people to resist the taxes that England was opposing.

The part of New England's militia called the minutemen were ready to fight at any moment.

organize a militia in Fairfax County, Virginia. They suggested that a local tax might be used to pay for it. They boldly and mockingly asked the sheriff to collect it for them, even though the sheriff was an appointee of Virginia's royal governor.

Henry's Call for War

The issue of public security was expected to be the topic of discussion when the House of Burgesses convened in 1775. Lord Dunmore, Virginia's royal governor, knew this. He was losing power, so he postponed calling the House of Burgesses into session. He pushed its meeting off until May. Peyton Randolph, the Speaker of the House of Burgesses who had helped to give Henry his lawyer's examination several years earlier, requested that the representatives meet in Richmond in late March to avoid interference from the royal governor and British troops. Although Henry, whose wife had died in February, was quite depressed, he traveled to Richmond.

Richmond was a small trading town. There, the delegates to the Virginia Convention met at the Henrico Parish Church. It was the only building in the town big enough to hold the 100 men who had traveled to Richmond.

Henry knew most of them. He had served with many of them in the House of Burgesses. Ten years before, he had argued against the Stamp Act with them. Travelers came from the far western reaches of the state, and Henry knew many of them, too.

The raucous mood was both belligerent (warlike) and optimistic. Adam Stephen, George Washington's former second in command in the army, bragged about what he would do if he met the royal governor. Rumors circulated about the business of the convention. Many thought that the convention should create its own provisional government. They wanted to levy (impose) taxes. None of the other states had gone that far. But, then, the time may have been right for such a move. Many thought that the king would punish them regardless of what they did. The petitions they had sent to England airing their grievances had done no good. They might as well go all the way and create their own government.

On the third day, Henry finally spoke. He sidestepped the issue of creating a government by proposing that the convention simply take it upon itself to organize a militia. "A well-regulated Militia composed of Gentlemen and Yeoman is the natural Strength and only Security of a free Government," his proposal read.

The debate began immediately. A lot of the delegates believed that Henry's proposal was going too far. For various reasons, they disagreed with Henry's push to go to war with England. Some were simply not as distrustful of the king as Henry was, and they believed that armed resistance was not necessary. They described Henry's proposal as being desperate. Others continued to hope for peace, arguing that, given more time, America's friends in Parliament could eventually reverse the policies. Others still were afraid to become entangled in a war in which they were sure that the British would crush the colonies.

Edmund Pendleton, the delegate from Caroline County, said: "We must arm, you say; but gentlemen must remember that blows are apt to follow the arming, and blood will follow blows, and sir, when this occurs the dogs of war will be loosed, friends will be converted into enemies, and this flourishing country will be swept with a tornado of death and destruction."

Henry knew he needed to speak out to defend his stance. He rose from his pew and walked to the front of the room. He began, "I have but one lamp by which my feet are guided and that is the lamp of experience." His voice lulled the men in the room into agreement. His oration skills were again a force of change. As he spoke, he spoke like a preacher, rousing his congregation to understand his point: in order to be free, the colonists must be ready to fight.

CHAPTER FOUR

THE FIGHT TO BE FREE

Henry was known as a rebel. However, here in Richmond at the Second Virginia Convention, in a stuffy church, amongst these lawmakers, he didn't want to be seen as someone who was going to recklessly rebel against England. He began his speech by saying he would be honest and he hoped no one would be offended by what he said. Henry understood the art of oration and wanted to assure his audience that he was a reasonable person. He felt passionately that the colonists would need to fight against England and so he continued his speech that conjured up many of the ideas America is founded on: freedom from oppression, freedom of speech, and liberty for everyone. Henry knew that the colonies could not be under English rule anymore, and that they would need to wage war in order to be their own country. He needed to convince the lawmakers in Richmond to take his side:

This is no time for ceremony. The question before the house is one of awful moment to this country. For my own part, I consider it as nothing less than a question of freedom or slavery; and in

This is an illustration of Patrick Henry giving his "Give Me Liberty or Give Me Death" speech at St. John's Church.

proportion to the magnitude of the subject ought to be the freedom of the debate. It is only in this way that we can hope to arrive at the truth, and fulfill the great responsibility which we hold to God and our country. Should I keep back my opinions at such a time, through fear of giving offense, I should consider myself as guilty of treason towards my country, and of an act of disloyalty toward the Majesty of Heaven, which I revere above all earthly kings.

This passage unveils several themes that are borne out in the rest of the speech. First, Henry likened the relationship

In the 18th century, slavery was common in the colonies. This illustration shows enslaved people on a tobacco farm around 1790.

between England and the colonies to slavery. This certainly echoed the sentiments of the colonists, who bristled at the British threat and use of force to impose policies in which they had no say. Further in the speech, Henry said, "Our chains are forged! Their clanging may be heard on the plains of Boston!" The slavery comparison is even more striking because slavery was legal and widely practiced in the colonies.

Henry's Conflicted Attitude Toward Slavery

Although Patrick Henry was the first Founding Father to demand freedom as an essential right for Americans, Henry owned slaves. However, he regarded slavery as a moral wrong. In a January 18, 1773, letter to abolitionist Quaker leader Robert Pleasants, he described slavery as a "lamentable evil" that he hoped would soon be abolished. He said he could not justify owning slaves, and yet he never set them free. Henry, who perplexingly used the argument of slavery against England, could not assert freedom for African American slaves in his own life.

The New Identity of the Colonists: Americans

Second, Henry used the terms "our country" and "my country" in referring to Virginia, in particular, and all the colonies in general. This clearly reflected the American identity that the colonists developed over time, especially in the years since Britain sought to tighten its control over them. As a result, Henry, like many of the colonists, found it easy to speak of a patriotism that was limited to the colonies and of treason that ignored the concerns of England.

Third, the passage, as does the rest of the speech, has a strong religious tone. This is in part a reflection of the influence of the revivalist preachers from Henry's youth. Also, it was common practice among public speakers of the time to invoke God to add credibility to their declarations. Moreover, there was a developing notion within the colonies that God had a special purpose for them. Henry later emphasized this notion when he declared, "There is a just God who presides over the destinies of nations, and who will raise up friends to fight our battles for us." He saw war with England not only as a patriotic act but also as a religious duty.

The Awful Moment

Henry then set about framing "the awful moment" that the colonies faced. He encouraged his colleagues to not give way to a false hope that the quarrel with England could be settled peacefully. For Henry, it was not an option to do nothing with the hope that things would somehow get better, especially when the actions of Great Britain over the previous ten years suggested that it intended to force the colonies into submission. Using a series of pointed rhetorical questions, Henry drove home his point:

Are fleets and armies necessary to a work of love and reconciliation? Have we shown ourselves so unwilling to be reconciled that force must be called in to win back our love? Let us not deceive ourselves, sir. These are the implements of war and subjugation; the last arguments to which kings resort. I ask gentlemen, sir,

King George III ruled in England from 1760 to 1820.

what means this martial array, if its purpose be not to force us to submission? Can gentlemen assign any other possible motive for it? Has Great Britain any enemy, in this quarter of the world, to call for all this accumulation of navies and armies? No, sir, she has none. They are meant for us: they can be meant for no other.

Henry also made it clear that the time for talking was over. He didn't see the value of continuing to reach out to England, when King George and Parliament were not receptive to the colonists' arguments. It was time for action.

There is no longer any room for hope. If we wish to be free . . . we must fight! . . . An appeal to arms and to the God of hosts is all that is left us! They tell us, sir, that we are weak; unable to cope with so formidable an adversary. But when shall we be stronger? Will it be the next week, or the next year? Will it be when we are totally disarmed, and when a British guard shall be stationed in every house? . . . Sir, we are not weak if we make a proper use of those means which the God of nature hath placed in our power. The millions of people, armed in the holy cause of liberty, and in such a country as that which we possess, are invincible by any force which our enemy can send against us.

Here, too, Henry addressed those representatives who feared going to war because they believed the colonies were no match for Britain's military power. He acknowledged the mismatch but felt that, with right and God on their side, the colonies could channel their anger and use their numbers and knowledge of the land to face down the British troops. He also felt that delaying action would only make the task harder. "There is no retreat, but in submission and slavery," he said.

In a masterful turn, Henry posed the most effective rhetorical question of his speech. "Is life so dear, or peace so sweet, as to be purchased at the price of chains and slavery?" It was a question that had only one reasonable or desirable answer. It need not have been answered, but Henry left no room for doubt. "Forbid it, Almighty God! I know not what course others may take; but as for me, give me liberty or give me death."

A Convinced Audience

Reports from the meeting said that as Henry delivered this famous closing line, he motioned as if driving a dagger into his heart. There was a stunned silence in the church. Henry had framed the most political issues in an intensely personal way. The silence lasted for several minutes. Debate soon resumed, but it was merely a formality. Henry's resolution passed by five votes. Henry was named the head of the militia committee. He and others, including Thomas Jefferson, had already concocted a plan. They submitted it to the convention the next morning.

Henry successfully used his rhetorical skills to convince the Second Virginia Convention. Around the country, other conventions were also realizing that war was on the horizon.

CHAPTER FIVE

THE LAND OF LIBERTY

Four weeks after Patrick Henry gave his speech, on an early April morning, shots were fired on the town green at Lexington, Massachusetts. Paul Revere had received word from the Sons of Liberty that the British army was planning to steal the colonists' weapons in a storehouse in Concord, Massachusetts. He quickly rode his horse to alert John Hancock, Samuel Adams and the minutemen, the local militia who were mostly farmers of Concord. In that early dawn, the minutemen took up their guns and met the British redcoats at the town green in Lexington. It's unknown who fired first, but the American Revolution had begun with "the shot heard 'round the world."

Rally Cry

Henry's words echoed across the land. "Give me liberty or give me death" became a rallying cry for men and women across the colonies. It was a powerful slogan that bridged two elements in society. For farmers and common citizens, it was a call to arms. It contained the pure conviction of being

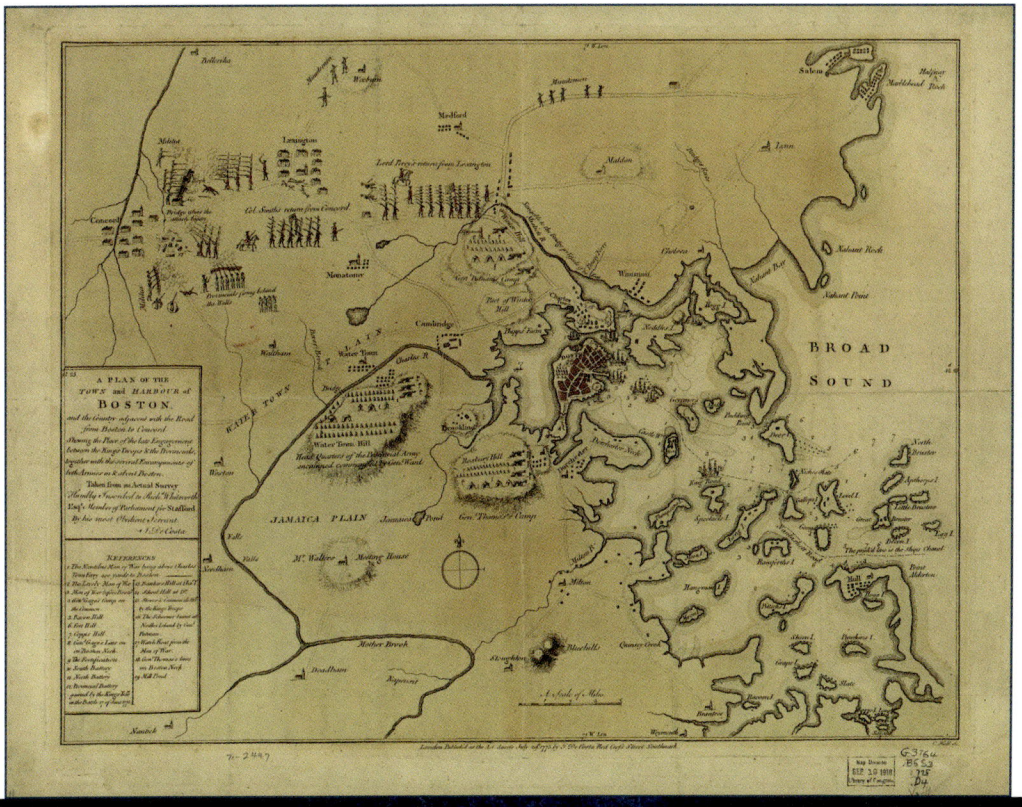

This map shows the battle of Lexington and Concord.

willing to die for one's beliefs. These were the men who would actually fight the Revolution. Many sewed the motto onto their ragged militia uniforms.

For politicians and scholars, it placed the focus on the meaning of liberty. "Liberty" is a vague term, but it was what they would be fighting for. There would be many intellectual battles about what, exactly, the word "liberty" meant. Around

US stamps printed from the 1960s have Patrick Henry's rally cry written on them.

the colonies, new local governments were springing up, openly defying British rule. Henry's phrase became the intellectual and moral fuel behind the revolutionary fire.

The Common Person

More and more frequently, the new local governments were comprised of regular workingmen. Politically, a new emphasis was placed on the individual or the common person. In this, an important shift in thinking occurred. Government did not grant liberty to its citizens. Liberty was inherent in the individual. Government's role, then, was to balance control in respect to the rights and liberties of its citizens. It was to serve the people, not the other way around. The idea that regular men should control the government was truly revolutionary. It shocked the British.

Throughout the colonies, local governments expressed this in varying ways. Some governments forwarded the idea of the secret ballot to maintain citizens' privacy. (Before that, much voting was done by a simple show of hands.) Many opened legislative meetings to the public. Likewise, many people now demanded public reporting of government business, such as publishing the minutes of meetings. Some demanded a public record of how their representatives voted.

Another shift occurred in the spread of information. Politicians once derived much of their knowledge by studying

Common Sense

During 1775 and 1776, the colonies were flooded with hundreds of pamphlets. Printing was cheap. Anybody who wanted to spread his ideas could do so. The most popular pamphlet was *Common Sense*, written by Thomas Paine. Like Henry, Paine made what had once been information for intellectuals into something accessible to the people. Paine used everyday language. He called King George a "royal brute." He quoted books everybody knew, such as the Bible. *Common Sense* became a popular discussion topic in taverns. More than 120,000 copies sold in less than three months. Paine showed that all that mattered in politics was the ability for one to think for oneself.

the great works of political philosophers such as John Locke and Niccolò Machiavelli. In the colonies, it became popular to distribute pamphlets.

The Second Continental Congress

In the late spring of 1776, the Second Continental Congress met in Philadelphia. There, Thomas Jefferson created a political document that articulated the unrest throughout the colonies. It was the Declaration of Independence. In 1,300 words, Jefferson framed these new thoughts of common liberty into a more formal political language. "We hold these truths to be self-evident, that all men are created equal," he wrote. Again, it was written from the perspective of the common man, as opposed to the government that looked over him.

Meanwhile, the war raged on. With Henry's saying, the Declaration of Independence, and the idea of liberty at their backs, George Washington and the Continental army pressed on. It was tough going. They suffered many setbacks. The British redcoats had an entire empire behind them. They were well trained and had ample supplies. Washington and his men were often working on the brink of starvation. "These are the times that try men's souls," Thomas Paine wrote.

Several times, Washington was almost forced to surrender, but he and his army persevered. The war reinforced the philosophical belief that the common man was just as good as the intellectual. Though the redcoats and their generals were professionally trained, they were not familiar with the American terrain. Militias from all over the colonies joined Washington's Continental army. Although his men were ragged, they knew

This painting shows the drafting of the Declaration of Independence.

the land. They had no problem hiding in bushes or scattering chaotically when needed.

Help from the French

The months stretched into years, with each side making numerous gains and beating hasty retreats. By 1780, the American army was on its last legs. Washington faced several mutinies. Soon, though, the Americans received military aid from the French navy. Throughout 1781, the Continental army won several decisive victories in the south. In October, British general Charles Cornwallis surrendered to Washington at Yorktown, Virginia. The American Revolution was over. The Americans had won.

Free at Last

The time had now come for self-government. The Articles of Confederation was the first American attempt to embody liberty in a system of government. It established the United States as a confederacy. The writers of the articles wanted liberty to be accounted for at every level. Thus, each state would remain sovereign (independent) from the others. The central government would have no power to tax the populace. In fact, its only function would be to provide for the nation's defense. The writers of the articles were so scared of the central government having too much power that they made it virtually powerless. The result was a continuation of the political chaos that had filled the colonies during war. Each state had its own currency, and banks and creditors printed their own money. The economic affairs of the fledgling United States were a mess.

The colonies had a difficult time transitioning from thirteen separate entities into the United States. There was some difficulty with federal and state division. Each state was expected to negotiate its own treaties with both foreign nations and native nations. The central government did not have enough money to create an army, thus the United States was confused and messy. The grand experiment was turning out to be a difficult balance. How much liberty was too much?

CHAPTER SIX

THE CONSTITUTION OF THE UNITED STATES OF AMERICA

The Articles of Confederation were not strong enough to hold this new nation together. America needed a new, stronger document that would set the ideals of the country. In 1787, the first Constitutional Convention was held in Philadelphia. The Founding Fathers would amend the Articles of the Confederation. This meant giving more power to a centralized government. Fear loomed—what if the new government took away the liberty they had just worked so hard to get?

In May 1787, fifty-five men descended on the Pennsylvania city and set to work. The men were predominantly upper class and almost universally well educated. They represented a small portion of American society and attempted to create a document that was capable of governing all.

This painting shows the signing of the US Constitution in 1787. This painting hangs in the US Capitol building.

The Virginia Plan vs. The New Jersey Plan

James Madison crafted the first proposal. It was known as the Virginia Plan. Under it, the United States would be reformed in a radical way. It would no longer be a confederacy of states. Rather, it would be a unified republic. Just as counties made up states, states would make up the nation. It would create an organized hierarchy of power. This was too much for some. The New Jersey Plan offered a counter-proposal that favored states' rights. It granted more power to the federal government, but each state would essentially remain an independent entity.

The Three Branches of Government

These were the terms of the debate. It raged over the summer and into early fall. Apparent stalemates were reached, and compromises were made. The resulting Constitution established three branches of federal government: the executive, legislative, and judicial. The executive branch, led by the president, would command the armed forces and control judiciary appointments. The legislative branch, comprised of Congress, would create laws. The judicial branch, led by the Supreme Court, would interpret the laws. An elaborate system of checks and balances was created, so that no branch could gain too much power.

The Constitution

The convention concluded in September. The Constitution had been written. Now it had to be presented to the individual states for approval. This would prove a challenge. The Constitution was a flawed document. Voting rights were extremely limited. Only one part of the federal government, the House of Representatives, would be determined by a simple popular election. The rest would be elected through a convoluted system of state legislatures.

Not All People Are Deemed Equal

More troubling was the fact that, in effect, the Constitution only represented a certain portion of the populace. The Constitution didn't explicitly exclude women, slaves, Indigenous persons, and men without property from voting. However, the state governments, led by the very men who drafted the Constitution, deprived these groups of the right to vote. In fact, despite the claim in the Declaration of Independence that "all men are created equal," women, slaves, and American Indians had virtually no rights in early America. Their exclusion from the Constitution was not surprising, even to its fiercest critics. To many, though, it was particularly bothersome.

Many feared the Constitution existed to serve its creators' interests. After all, if only men with property could vote, then how would men without property be represented? Many resented this. It created a division between rich and poor, and it made the poor powerless. In fact, the Constitution itself did very little to protect the rights of its citizens.

The Federalist Papers

Twelve years earlier, colonies had met to form militias. Now, as states, they met to ratify, or approve, the Constitution. The debate raged across the United States. Those in favor of the constitution were known as the Federalists. Those against it, such as Henry, were known as the Anti-Federalists. Alexander Hamilton, James Madison, and John Jay—some of the Constitution's creators—published an anonymous series of articles in New York newspapers. They became known as the Federalist papers. They laid out the basic terms of the debate. Once again, Henry became the champion of the people. He was one voice out of many, but his was a loud and well-spoken one.

A New Democracy

Patrick Henry was troubled by the new Constitution. Though it began with the phrase "We the people," Henry saw little reason to believe that the Constitution was for "the people." It was for the states, he argued. Ultimately, he believed, the result would be a tyrannical government and a powerless citizenry. Even its very creation was a sign of tyranny, he claimed. The framers of the Constitution had met in Philadelphia to fix the Articles of Confederation, not create a whole new government! "The people gave them no power to use their name!" he complained at the Virginia ratification convention in June 1788.

Still a Songbird of the People

The Virginia ratification convention was filled with political stars. In addition to Henry, there were James Madison, Benjamin Harrison, James Monroe, Richard Henry Lee, George Mason, and others in attendance. George Washington remained at home at Mount Vernon, though he communicated with the convention daily through letters. It was clear from the outset that the debate would not be easy. Though Henry's health was declining, he remained the center of attention. His powers of rhetoric had not diminished.

The convention was filled with drama. Some high-profile politicians, such as Virginia governor Edmund Randolph, switched their positions from Federalist to Anti-Federalist. Henry declared that the Constitution lacked a basic bill of rights. While there were checks and balances in the system, they acted only between the states and the federal government. A bill of rights would protect the rights of individuals. Nobody disagreed.

Bill of Rights

Henry argued that the Constitution should be rewritten. His opponents argued that it should be ratified and amended later. Henry didn't see the point. To approve an arrangement, then specify the details seemed illogical to him. The debate continued. Both Henry and his opponents introduced items they wished to see included in a bill of rights. They soon voted on whether to ratify the Constitution. The results were 89–79 in favor of the Constitution. However, the delegates also passed a declaration of rights, predominantly penned by Henry. It included the right to free speech and the right to bear arms, and it prevented the government from forcing citizens to house soldiers in their homes.

These articles were adopted during the first session of the US Congress. They became the basis for the first ten amendments to the Constitution. They are a testament to the power of Patrick Henry. Though he was not the sole architect of the Bill of Rights by any means, he was the main force behind its rapid adoption.

Patrick Henry was able to use language, his voice, and the art of rhetoric to convince the colonists that they could have their own democracy, independent of England. He continued to be a voice of rebellion, on the side of liberty and someone who championed the Bill of Rights, a document which today we believe gives liberty to all people in this, our idea that turned into a country.

PRIMARY SOURCE TRANSCRIPTIONS

"Give Me Liberty or Give Me Death"

No man thinks more highly than I do of the patriotism, as well as abilities, of the very worthy gentlemen who have just addressed the house. But different men often see the same subject in different lights; and, therefore, I hope it will not be thought disrespectful to those gentlemen if, entertaining as I do opinions of a character very opposite to theirs, I shall speak forth my sentiments freely and without reserve. This is no time for ceremony. The question before the house is one of awful moment to this country. For my own part, I consider it as nothing less than a question of freedom or slavery; and in proportion to the magnitude of the subject ought to be the freedom of the debate. It is only in this way that we can hope to arrive at the truth, and fulfill the great responsibility which we hold to God and our country. Should I keep back my opinions at such a time, through fear of giving offense, I should consider myself as guilty of treason towards my country, and of an act of disloyalty toward the Majesty of Heaven, which I revere above all earthly kings.

Mr. President, it is natural to man to indulge in the illusions of hope. We are apt to shut our eyes against a painful truth, and listen to the song of that siren till she transforms us into beasts. Is this the part of wise men, engaged in a great and arduous struggle for liberty? Are we disposed to be of the numbers of those who, having eyes, see not, and, having ears, hear not, the things which so nearly concern their temporal salvation? For my part, whatever anguish of spirit it may cost, I am willing to know the whole truth, to know the worst, and to provide for it.

I have but one lamp by which my feet are guided, and that is the lamp of experience. I know of no way of judging of the future but by the past. And judging by the past, I wish to know what there has been in the conduct of the British ministry for the last ten years to justify those hopes with which gentlemen have been pleased to solace themselves and the House. Is it that insidious smile with which our petition has been lately received?

Trust it not, sir; it will prove a snare to your feet. Suffer not yourselves to be betrayed with a kiss. Ask yourselves how this gracious reception of our petition comports with those warlike preparations which cover our waters and darken our land.

There is no longer any room for hope. If we wish to be free—if we mean to preserve inviolate those inestimable privileges for which we have been so long contending—if we mean not basely to abandon the noble struggle in which we have been so long engaged, and which we have pledged ourselves never to abandon until the glorious object of our contest shall be obtained—we must fight! I repeat it, sir, we must fight! An appeal to arms and to the God of hosts is all that is left us! They tell us, sir, that we are weak; unable to cope with so formidable an adversary. But when shall we be stronger? Will it be the next week, or the next year? Will it be when we are totally disarmed, and when a British guard shall be stationed in every house? Shall we gather strength but irresolution and inaction? Shall we acquire the means of effectual resistance by lying supinely on our backs and hugging the delusive phantom of hope, until our enemies shall have bound us hand and foot? Sir, we are not weak if we make a proper use of those means which the God of nature hath placed in our power. The millions of people, armed in the holy cause of liberty, and in such a country as that which we possess, are invincible by any force which our enemy can send against us. Besides, sir, we shall not fight our battles alone. There is a just God who presides over the destinies of nations, and who will raise up friends to fight our battles for us. The battle, sir, is not to the strong alone; it is to the vigilant, the active, the brave. Besides, sir, we have no election. If we were base enough to desire it, it is now too late to retire from the contest. There is no retreat but in submission and slavery! Our chains are forged! Their clanking may be heard on the plains of Boston! The war is inevitable—and let it come! I repeat it, sir, let it come.

It is in vain, sir, to extenuate the matter. Gentlemen may cry, Peace, Peace—but there is no peace. The war is actually begun! The next gale that sweeps from the north will bring to our ears the clash of resounding arms! Our brethren are already in the field! Why stand we here idle? What is it that gentlemen wish? What would they have? Is life so dear, or peace so sweet, as to be purchased at the price of chains and slavery? Forbid it, Almighty God! I know not what course others may take; but as for me, give me liberty or give me death!

CHRONOLOGY

1736 Patrick Henry is born.

1745 George Whitefield travels through Hanover County, Virginia.

1760 Henry becomes a lawyer.

1763 The French and Indian War ends. Henry argues the Parson's Cause case.

1764 England passes the Sugar Act and the Currency Act.

1765 England passes the Stamp Act and the Quartering Act. Henry joins the House of Burgesses.

1766 The Declaratory Act is passed.

1770 The Boston Massacre takes place.

1773 The Boston Tea Party takes place.

1774 England passes the Coercive Acts. The First Continental Congress is convened.

1775 Henry delivers his "Give Me Liberty or Give Me Death" speech at the Virginia Convention. The American Revolution begins.

1776 The Declaration of Independence is signed. Thomas Paine publishes *Common Sense*.

1781 England surrenders to the Continental army at Yorktown, Virginia. The American Revolution ends.

1787 The Constitutional Convention convenes in Philadelphia. The battle for ratification ensues.

1791 The Bill of Rights is ratified.

1799 Patrick Henry dies.

GLOSSARY

abolitionist A person who championed anti-slavery.

Anti-Federalist One in opposition to the Constitution and in favor of a confederate government.

apprentice A person who learns a trade by working for an experienced person.

belligerent Hostile or inclined to wage war.

confederacy A form of government comprised of smaller, mostly independent states.

Federalist One in support of the Constitution and in favor of a republican government.

itinerant Constantly traveling.

loom A machine that turned wool or thread into cloth.

militia An army comprised of private citizens.

oration Speech delivered in a formal manner.

pamphlet A small publication of limited distribution.

republic A form of government elected by individual citizens.

sovereign Independent.

specie Money that is coins rather than paper.

tyrant One who exhibits absolute control unjustly.

BIBLIOGRAPHY

Andrews, Evan. "Patrick Henry's 'Liberty or Death' Speech."
     History.com. March 22, 2015. https://www.history.com/
     news/patrick-henrys-liberty-or-death-speech-
     240-years-ago.

Beard, Charles A. *An Economic Interpretation of the
     Constitution of the United States.* New York, NY: The
     Free Press, 1941.

Bowen, Catherine Drinker. *Miracle at Philadelphia: The
     Story of the Constitutional Convention, May to
     September 1787*. Boston, MA: Back Bay Books, 1966.

Cavallo, Dominick. *A Fiction of the Past: The Sixties in
     American History*. New York, NY: Palgrave Books, 1999.

Grote, JoAnn A. *Patrick Henry: American Statesman and
     Speaker*. Philadelphia, PA: Chelsea House Publishers,
     2000.

Hamilton, Alexander, John Jay, and James Madison. *The
     Federalist Papers*. Garry Wills, ed. New York, NY:
     Bantam Books, 1982.

Inge, M. Thomas, ed. *Concise Histories of American
     Popular Culture*. Westport, CT: Greenwood Publishing
     Group, 1982.

Marston, Daniel. *The American Revolution, 1774–1783
     (Essential Histories)*. Oxford, England: Osprey Press,
     2002.

Mayer, Henry. *A Son of Thunder: Patrick Henry and the American Republic*. Charlottesville, VA: University Press of Virginia, 1991.

Murphy, Sharon Ann. "History of Money in America: What Colonists Used as Currency." *Time*. February 27, 2017. http://time.com/4675303/money-colonial-america-currency-history.

"The Sons of Liberty." Ushistory.org. Retrieved March 6, 2019. http://www.ushistory.org/declaration/related/sons.html.

Wood, Gordon S. *The American Revolution: A History.* New York, NY: The Modern Library, 2002.

Wright, Mike. *What They Didn't Teach You About the American Revolution.* Novato, CA: Presidio Press, 1999.

Zinn, Howard. *A People's History of the United States*. New York, NY: HarperCollins, 1999.

FURTHER READING

Books

Atkinson, Rick. *The British Are Coming: The War for America, Lexington to Princeton, 1775-1777*. New York, NY: Henry Holt and Company, 2019.

Casey, Susan. *Women Heroes of the American Revolution: 20 Stories of Espionage, Sabotage, Defiance, and Rescue*. Chicago, IL: Chicago Review Press, 2017.

Hinderaker, Eric. *Boston's Massacre*. Cambridge, MA: Harvard University Press, 2019.

Kukla, Jon. *Patrick Henry: Champion of Liberty*. New York, NY: Simon and Schuster Paperbacks, 2017.

Paine, Thomas, and Alan Dershowitz. *Common Sense: And Other Writings*. New York, NY: Skyhorse, 2019.

Websites

The Colonial Williamsburg Foundation
www.history.org
This website has information about concepts and history relating to the American Revolution.

Independence Hall
www.nps.gov/inde
This website is about Independence Hall, which is now a National Park.

Patrick Henry: Bill of Rights Institute

billofrightsinstitute.org/educate/educator-resources/founders/patrick-henry

This page includes history and educational resources relating to Patrick Henry's life.

Patrick Henry National Memorial

www.redhill.org

This website is about Patrick Henry's personal history and his last residence, Red Hill.

INDEX